POETRY BY ANTONIA WANG:

IN ENGLISH:

Love Bites: Poetry & Prose (2019)
In the Posh Cocoon: Poetry and Bits of Life (2020)
Hindsight 2020: Brief Reflections on a Long Year (2021)
Palette: Love Poems and Painted Words (2022)
Things I Could Have Said in One Line But Didn't: Poems on Love,
Relationships and Existentialism (2023)

IN SPANISH:

Retrospectiva 2020: Reflexiones breves sobre un año largo (2021)
Matices: Poemas de amor y paisajes del alma (2023)
Rincones barridos: Poesías del interior (2023)

taste of
salt

Poems by Antonia Wang

FIRST EDITION

Paperback ISBN: 979-8-9860457-9-5
Ebook ISBN: 979-8-9903875-0-8

Written by Antonia Wang
Edited by Vanessa Anderson

www.biteslove.com

The following poems
were crafted between 2007 and 2018.
Dedicated with love and gratitude
to the people and places
that inspired them.

To my readers:
May you find joy, solace, and strength
within these verses.

Contents

I gift you a box of memories,
amalgam of lives,
souvenirs picked by owls—
who aren't here.
Fresh realities ring surreal
on my right ear.
My heart lags behind a brain
primed for change,
seeking solace every minute.
Grasping is inane.

"Sweet Realities," Love Bites

Taste of Salt

You won't recall the things I gave you,
but those I didn't take away.
Not that I gave you freedom,
but I did not clip your wings.

You won't dwell on the laughs I caused,
but on the wounds I left intact.
You'll notice the messy rooms I didn't touch,
the gopher holes I didn't fill,
the hot meals I didn't cook—
the fragile dishes I did not break.

You will wish that was me, tossing a spatula
across the room… stirring the pot.
Instead, there will be stillness,
and simplicity in the way
I brushed past your life
leaving ripples but no marks;
taking nothing but what I brought,
and your memories, and your salt.

You might argue that's a stain.
I would venture you've been primed.
Listen carefully, that's the silence
of me gone from your life—
nothing showing, just knowing smiles,
and the quenching taste of salt.

The Haunting

We mourn this loss, as it cowers
under the shadow of "could have been"—
far from the oases we might have shared,
blurred by connections on another plane.

I wander this desert, lucid, and observe
a tinge of regret within your gaze,
pleas for understanding on your face,
the depths of longing in your days.

The path we chose not to tread
threatens to haunt us both.
In dreams, we regress to might-have-beens,
and wake up to the truth of "never was."

What I Gave You

What I gave you were crumbs of love—
passion the wolves didn't devour.
What I sought in you were tender hugs,
bites from a fruit time hadn't soured.

And I did not gift you any rocks
to seal our solemn commitment.
There was no white dress billowing
in the Caribbean Sea breeze.

What we shared was a certainty
beyond wishful fabrication.
We inhaled the air of tranquility,
hands entwined in mutual recognition.

Love, as we knew it, had come and gone.
No sighs, no tears, no shock.

In sobriety, from that fading high,
I came to know you, steadfast
like a leaf in the wind—
clear as the water on our untouched shore.

What I gave you was me, and I am no gift.

Gardenias and Toothpicks

A smile, an encounter, an open mind...
A wisp of gardenia off the menu.
Six-foot-two? I ask (an inside joke).
Sharp mind, soft hands, touch of heavens...
Keep speaking, you're captivating,
shed those layers.

Can I watch you practice yoga?
May I join you for dinner?
Shall I brew your tea?
Two looming tempests,
seated across the table...
The full moon transforms you into a wolf,
and I want to be ravaged
but will settle for a hug.

What is that fragrance? Gardenias?
I'll carry the aroma in my car.
Can I see you? Nerves burst like fireflies.
Now? We have an abundance of time.
You speak, I listen, and become entranced.
Catalog... tailor-made...
It was you then, and so it was.

Guitars and Drums

You set the tone; I bring the soul.
Your jams are boundless and I enjoy.

I join your band and improvise
a senseless song *en español*.

You think it's cute, but I'm just buzzed.
You look at me with impure thoughts,

biting your lips, I'm reduced to meat.
You smile in secrecy, your face so sweet.

Sit on my rug, watch me undress.
I want to sleep, and you're upset.

You hope and pray you get your way.
Sooner or later, aware or not,

I dance to your tunes, sing to your songs.
Not much to ponder, a world to explore.

For you're the guitar, and I'm the drums.

Bird House

When the music stops,
there is a dreadful silence.
Someone who only echoes you is hollow.

Blissful moments cannot be cloned.
It is unjust to gauge the present
with yesterday's tape.

This ill-fitting dress is all I own.
To not wear it is to be exposed.
Why reveal skin no one will touch?

Why *have* skin when I can't feel?
There is a birdhouse for sale.
I think I might buy it to shelter my soul.

Early Whispers

Life happened,
and I forgot your skin—
shimmering silk yogurt,
endless…

I forgot the taste of bliss,
and a muted breath
reclaimed the silence.

One day, I woke up
with a ring on my finger.
You whispered,
"we should be together,"
but *'should be'* left me adrift.

Should broken birds fly solo?
Should infants be left alone?
Should I respond to your words
with words?

Life happened, and you forgot.
You forgot, and life happened.

I prefer it this way.
Last time you happened,
it was life I forgot.

Ode to Impermanence

Sway to the bittersweet ballad,
beautiful things reaching their end.
Melding joy with the tune of sorrow—
a parting presence that lingers
as you bid them farewell…

Dance to the beat of impermanence;
a delight of tears in a static embrace.
The refuge of love, the comfort of pain
wedged in your heart
with each beginning and every end.

Good Samaritan

I dreamed a dream where you stalled,
avoiding an encounter with truth,
seeking solace in dissatisfaction
with someone else.

I wonder what crosses your mind
at this very moment; what you would say
if I were inanimate, never to respond—
what steps you would take without fear.

You carry your wounds with pride,
walking about just to prove
your threshold for pain.

I sense the void of your inner anguish,
and wander, helpless, for I can't help you.

Against the Current

If there is an after life, then live.
If this is all there is, all the more reason to live.
If the days are slowing down, pause.
If the wheels keep on spinning, go on living.

Live as though there is no impeding twilight;
whether the river flows or floods,
whether fires burn, if storms destroy,
and if the earth quakes.
Live, as if there is no death,
even if tomorrow marks the end.

Experience the frisson of cool water on a
scorching summer day, the warmth of flesh,
a child's hug, the vibrant nature, the red.
Live, as though there are no cynics
attempting to wake you from your cheerful
reverie. Savor watching fruit grow,
relish simple things.

Live intensely, whether life is a mere figment
or the only fact. Grasp the evasive truth,
hug your only friend—a most profound
revelation: this moment, this instant…
whether it lasts a second, or an eternity.

Taste of Salt

Mother Prison

Mother prison for over eight billion souls…
Beyond your waters, space is our wall.
An army of sleepers calls you a stage.
Most of them dream, a few are awake,
taking fragile avatars for a ride
in a quantum slumber, we call life.

Like most mothers who share your shame,
you take no credit and all of the blame.
Lucid dreamers know to design
masterpieces, with you aligned.
Those with amnesia forget it's a ride,
puzzled by barriers and wants that collide.

Mother prison, I dream awake.
Let me paint a masterpiece no one will notice.
For everyone's busy, weaving
their own dreams, conducting concertos
in symphonies of "seem."

And when I finish dreaming
this last dream of mine,
please let me be home
at *Is-Be*,[1] my land.

---

[1] Inspired by the book "Alien Interview" by Lawrence Spencer.

Electricity and Hope

"Absence makes the heart grow fonder—"
or weary, or hopeless. Seconds are tallied,
dreaded, resented (for you are not *here*).

There exists a sadistic lottery of which
you are a winner, and by default, so am I.
Let us count our blessings.

Absence is a quest for normalcy, measured
in waves of sadness, and impotence,
electricity and hope.

Counting life by the seconds… you are *here*,
making up for moments lost. Life… interrupted,
upheld by the courage of love.

To be present, in this moment, is all I ask.
My ambition is a day, a week, a month
with my perfect love, in this flawed body.

A chaotic world, sans-Absence…[2]

---

[2] For children suffering from Childhood Absence Epilepsy, and the
people who love them.

Taste of Salt

Bayou Con Dios

You departed swamp lands in search of brighter scenery. Alligators with mouths agape craved your joy.

In that murky water, you left your shackles, tears, and filth. Lighter now, you seek rest on a white sand beach.

You shed your body, but the energetic junk still lingers, haunting you and everyone else.

The water is alluring, but the waves will cast you out. There is no perfect beach on this continent.

Yemaya[3] is livid, but she still cleanses you. It is so bright out here! You are purified by quartz and sea salt.

Walk to that emerald ocean and become one with your element. The muck has vanished.

In this land of bayous, *vaya con Dios.*

---

[3] Yemoja, Yemaya, or Lemanya: water goddess in Afro-Caribbean and syncretic traditions.

Love and Concentration Camps

....

What good is living
when you are no longer needed?

It is true, nobody needs you,
but are you loved?

Ah, you lost the capacity
for unconditional love.

Feelings did not survive
the Concentration Camps.

What horrors lie dormant
in the human mind,

inside barb-wired shadows
that steel the heart.

Your reptilian needs are
covered, thankfully.

Your high intellect was
cultivated, skillfully.

But the elusive emotions,
the ones you cast aside,

akin to those of dogs...
they torment you.

Dogs sense days in advance
their companion's time to die.

Can you grasp your own fragility?
As your time draws near,

what do you seek if not
companionship,

the embrace of friends,
old and new—

perhaps those of lesser intellect?
You no longer mind.

Even a store clerk will do.
When no one needs you,

> *what good are pennies,*
> *knowledge,*

> *if all you desire is touch,*
> *if you would travel*

> *across the country*
> *for a hug?*

Your body decays,
yet your spirit soars.

You know this.
You have the drive

of five young men.
So, you drive.

Alcohol may still your thoughts,
but what will soothe you?

> *Love is the loftier mind.*
> *It always has been.*

> *Need becomes irrelevant*
> *when love exists.*

Stay for coffee.
You are no bother.

You are not needed,
but you are loved.

> *If only you understood*
> *that you are love.*

Scarcity does not apply.
Come back and visit.
> *Love is always in supply.*[4]

---

[4] In Memoriam: W.H.

Hide and Seek

Where did you vanish that hazy Sunday morning?
What new toy lured you into a treacherous maze?
Who entwines your legs on brisk, sun-starved hours?
Who's seen my love? Where is my love?

Where did you go when you left me shattered?
Who cast you away, why aren't we together?
Why does emptiness brim in this wobbling cup?
Who stole my soul? Where hides my soul?

Big round eyes watched me through framed art,
donning sunflowers, and honeyed skin—
watermelons on their heads spewing sardonic jests.
Who usurps my home? Where is my home?

They brewed tea on this cool, moonlit night,
urging me to remember how it felt to stand alone.
Then left me wordless, in gaslit solitude—
bewildering, hushed, surreal.
The intoxicating wisp of background Marley
chimed: "No Woman, No Cry."

They asked me to recall inner quietude
while my spirit grappled with itself.
You must retrieve what my mind erased.
Who sings my song? What is my song?

And you left as you arrived: unassuming, serene.

The face I thought I knew, wearing newfound smiles...
That a rose is a rose,[5] but why wilt so soon?
My carefree love, forever lost.

---

[5] Reference to Mecano's song: *Una rosa es una rosa* (A Rose Is a Rose)

Taste of Salt

Reach

My flesh lacks skin—
wounds unhealed, unscabbed.
That subtle scratch
you didn't make,
continues to bleed.

You extend your hand across the table,
(the one that's wise).
It purges the grime and weaves me,
with compassion, a resilient skin.

Transparent, yet resolute,
it unfurls, from fingertips to toes,
radiant with warmth,
sealed with a glow.

Extend your hand, and we'll leap
with unwavering confidence.
Reach across the table.

Embrace my pain,
that I may stand exposed,
with wounds still gushing,
and flesh laid bare,
at ease, before you.

In Color

Roses disrobe their yellow whims,
while my heart is cloaked in blue.
With each artful touch of your hands,
harmonious ripples vibrate within,
in unfolding waves of white and pink.

In the quiet moments, it's you—
a flickering light at midnight.
In every surge of passion, a striking red…
a subtle palette of tears and smiles,
glazing this land with hopeful greens.

From the Inside Out

If I implored you to cease,
you would persist, flaunting
your ebony body and wings of dawn.

If I begged you not to intrude,
you would paralyze me, still—
my web woven of wit offers no defense.

Your non-venom, strangely warm,
courses within, transporting me
to an unclaimed heaven where pain eludes,
anguish dissolves, hunger fades,
fear dissipates.

If I could entreat you to halt, I surmise,
you wouldn't retreat, seeking another refuge.
You lay them upon me, and I remain unmoved,
incapable of feeling, objecting, accepting—
only observing.

I wait, and reciprocally, so do you, so do they.
You for yours, yours for theirs, and I for yours
to mature, hatch and feast on my living flesh,
devouring me from the inside out.[6]

---

[6] Of the tarantula hawk and its prey…

Look for You

The city hums with dirt and sound,
helmets and feet, and I search for you.

I seek you out, knowing precisely where
you are, aware your life is off-limits,
and your heart was never mine.

Renaissance flower children… I see them
everywhere, with their urban dreams
and slender frames. You wander lost,
seeking unburied treasure, striving to become.

I look for you, as if peering through glass
at a colony of ants, observable but beyond
understanding.

I strain to hear the ring of truth, dulled by fire
sirens, and find it rendered on a mural.

For the bliss we shared was a chimera,
existing only as abstract art—where you once
questioned if you could trust, and I could try.

I search for you, certain there is nothing
to look at, for, or forward to.

In the Silence, I Find

I.
I have found it, and it flows like a river—
its deep waters calmly pooling downstream.

I have found it, clear stream running,
life abounds beneath my fingertips.

I have found it, even from afar,
its memory brings a smile—

a personal haven, a lasting respite.
No need to own, for how can one possess

immensity and beauty?
This bliss is meant to be shared.

Omnipresent, my days are watermarked
with its golden seal.

Yet, once I turn the page,
it leaves no trace.

I have found it, and now I see,
there is nothing quite like this.

No passion compares, no obsession withstands.
Only freedom can touch this joy.

Like a dove in my hands,
this love is to catch and release.

II.
It holds no object or subject in its grip,
and claims no one, but reaches all who seek it.

It yields no anxiety, wants, or waits.
It is peace, assurance, and awareness.

No prisoners within, for it is not a prison—
a condition that liberates, an impulse to create.

Without boundaries, for it is not a place.
It has no pursuits, save the tick of now.

The unending grace never departs.
Emerges from thin air and fills up my life.

I summoned it with a heart-sung prayer,
impatient stars swirling my rustic wand.

I wanted better and longed for more.
Now that I have it, there is no craving.

It finds me when I'm ready, oh, glorious jaunt!
It doesn't knock; it comes in quietly.

Suddenly, it is there, healing wounds,
brightening the space.

I gaze upon it, no need for inquiry.
I acknowledge the fulfillment of my desires.

Finally here, experienced in sheer wonder;
before uttering a word, I sense its might.

I am ready, and I know this is my gift,
my blessed gift of peace, a soulful uplift.

Leaving me tamed, poised, and prepared
to give myself as I haven't done.

It gives only what it takes. It takes only what it gives.
It gives and takes only what it is.

It knows no object; it needs no subject—
a timeless presence that always dwells within.

Divine

You glisten, pearly skin aglow,
almost translucent, as your eyes—
entrance with mystic ocean depth.

A tranquil radiance traces your aura.
Your form, a candid lotus unfolding,
humble shoulders, and crystalline mind.

Where do you come from?
Who is your family?
What does Earth mean to your kind?
What architect outlined your soul
and sequenced your DNA?

How do you find our sun-kissed planet,
and is your purpose to shine?
Because you glimmer before me
ever so brightly, like life itself—
so light, so calm.

Estranged Family

Sister, I've known you long.
Quisqueya[7] birthed us both.
You were a rebel of youth.
I learned some tricks from you.

You are free from oppression. I, from you.
We went our separate ways,
and occasionally engaged in cat fights.
It didn't matter who was right.

Sister, a Massacre divides us.
You are safe from intrusion.
I, safe from your pain.

For you have been beaten,
violated, desecrated and ignored
more than I know.

A knot gathers in my throat
every time I hear of you.
Unexplainable sorrow imbues my blood.

Sister, the H is silent, and so are your aches.
"Nou se mond la, nou se timoun yo."
Let them hear your cries.

---

[7] Quisqueya (Kiskeya): native Taino name for the island of Hispaniola
(shared by the Dominican Republic and Haiti), believed to mean
"mother of all lands."

Let them clean your wounds,
so you can find your way.

How can you be lost in such a small land?
Quisqueya hears you. Quisqueya heals you.

Wipe off your tears, so you can see
from greater heights, from loftier sights
what you can be, Haiti.

The Scale

Before you engage in games,
ponder if you can afford to lose.
Love is a capricious maiden.
Embrace her while she desires you.

Before you presume I'm a given,
know I am a moon-child.
Would nights be as bright without me?
Will you harbor no regrets?

Before you play with fire,
remember I am a dragon,
and my mouth remains closed to spare you
agony; but if it's fire you want…

Before you abduct your feelings,
consider the look in your eyes
on that beach, that July.
Those eyes questioned what I saw in you,
whether I loved you back.
And you're still wondering, reluctant to see
that the answer was yes, then and now.

Before you feel assured,
recall we met on a trail.
I passed you by as you sat,
then returned to claim you.
You linger where I left you.

No one else has come for you,
including yourself.

Before trusting your fears,
heed your intuition.
Your mind broke your heart
and it seeks to blame me.

Before your ego runs rampant,
contemplate what's at stake.
Measure what your pride is worth.
While it's true I love you better,
it is evident you love me more.

Venus Second Dance

Silent bliss, being next to…
I crave nothing more than moments
like this, under the sun, gazing at the sky
over a hollow log.

Chalk rainbows grace the pavement
with hues of orange, and shirts—
with shades of blue, and flip-flops.

"I like you," you said, as though it were a gift.
A gift of lust, spontaneity, and free-falling,
falling in love, with little things,
with tiny cheesecakes…

Meister of funk,
sharp scissors target your wings.
You'd better go. Polish those tunes,
fly where you please.

Though plenty of fun, it came
at the expense of liberties untold.
Entiendo, amor.
I hope you encountered what you sought.

Stay unbound, to jump and play,
to ride and sing. Hope you've found joy
in the kind of love that sets you free.

Give me one more dance
on that grand stage cycling the sun.
Let me smile again and look in your eyes
as I did the first time.

I'll tell you I still know what I knew
back then, *y a lo mejor sabrás:*
as rare as watching Venus swing by,
our fleeting love was a precious find.

Metaphor

I greet you with a smile, my dearest love.
You seep timidly through my window,
like a ray of light, guide me
to a luscious garden where joy hides
behind greens and flowers, water and life.

The colors, all you, oh precious eyes!
A mild breeze on my face,
a deep, calm breath, and a lingering thrill.
You are the early silence before the rain,
the fragrant meadows where we embrace.

I welcome you with adolescent giggles,
oh butterfly! A prayer, a fluttering hymn,
a grin on my face—a ballad,
an indulgent daydream,
a sigh on my frosted skin,
the rose to which life blushes
before she swirls and spins.

I anoint you with honey, my sweetest one.
You are the wind, you are the wind,
and you can blow. Blow my way!
Envelop me, perfect as you will ever be—
with young and supple skin,
wisdom's emissary who found a home.
A flower, you're an orchid. Extend your stay.
Beauty is in no rush where you emanate.

Every story has a feeling
looming behind the chest.
You're the heart-breaker, and heart mender
in my wild west.

You are the sage that sowed the garden,
drew the birds, and opened the cage.
You are the steer that bred with valor
and tilled a once sterile earth.
You are the brush that beautifies.
You are the hands that sketched the sky.

May our paths be one.
May I serve your morning coffee.
May I sleep to your caress.
May I gaze fondly at your face.
May your perfect body age with grace.
May your wild spirit remain untamed.
May your brilliance linger
on my bedroom window.

And if our journeys were to fork,
may glorious be life, and exalted be love!
May only daisies adorn your path.
May peace be your companion,
loyal and steadfast.
May you embody joy.
May your orchids last.
May their sepals glow
when the night contrasts.

May you walk on petals,
and glisten in the snow.
May your essence shine
for all to know.
May you be abundant,
and soar lightly, oh dove!

May your life be brightened,
as you have lit my own.
May we meet anew,
may I find your gaze.
May we color the sky,
as we glide and alight
on that cloud,
at the end of the rainbow.[8]

---

[8] Reference to Ricardo Montaner's song: Al final del arcoiris (At the End of the Rainbow).

Cat Fight

Life and I got into an argument.
I called her neglectful; she called me needy.
I called her stingy; she called me wasteful.
I called her insensitive; she called me touchy.

I said, "You fell short!"
She countered, "Get over it."
I called her cavalier; she called me serious.
I called her careless; she winked:
"Live a little." I called her immature;
she dared "You should try it."
I called her overrated; she called me bitter.

"You think you're all that!" I reproached.
"And you think you're not!"
She grabbed my hair; I seized her wrists
and threatened to throw her off a cliff.

"I'm yours to throw."
"Want some take out?" I said.
"And beer after."
"You're a piece of work."
"You're a prize yourself.
Now, get me off this cliff, it's cold!"

We kissed and made up.

If Eminem Were Zen

If Eminem were Zen,
what would he rap about then?

Would we hear all the slander
if there weren't any anger?

Would he give fans such a thrill
without threatening to kill?

Would he still be Slim Shady
if he started chanting daily?

Eminem, multi-platinum:

If you shed the pain facade,
would you still be a rap god?

If your light shone through in peace,
would your earnings then decrease?

Would you give it all away
if it meant you found your way?

If you learned what makes you grim,
would you stop trashing Kim?

Would people buy your albums
if "Om" replaced your stardom?

As your songs blast berserk
I just wonder with a smirk:

Will hip hop ever lose its gem
to an enlightened Eminem?

Moving Mountains

Love gave us wings
and tethered our feet.

I dream of you at times,
but my dreams won't humor me.

We stand miles apart,
in both distance and thought.

We met at a fork,
and you chose your path.

I carried your ghost,
like a stain in my heart.

I journey in peace
yearning for the day

when on that hollow log,
we'll share a gaze at the stars.

Blissful…
in spite of you, in spite of me.

Mountains may converge,
triggering earthquakes as they collide.

Iron & Wine

Your music became my lullaby, Iron & Wine.
On these lonesome, wind-whooped nights,
a consoling hand stroking my head,
serenading me to sleep under shy stars.

And upon waking, sepia visions
of a small Madera room…
Our backs languid on the warm floor,
those restless hours, the ceaseless chatter,
the sultry sighs, the swift reveal
of warm bodies and bare souls.

Your mellow tunes are now my lullabies,
Iron & Wine, guiding me through slumber
to a sweet remembrance.

Falling

Mix water and oil.

Dirt rises, clouding the stream,
while your belly of silk caresses me
from behind, like a hand cradling a rose.

Cause mayhem.

Put me on that roller coaster
I wish not to ride.
You find it intriguing—
the places I've been, the stories I tell.
I live for the present, and the person I was
remains in those moments.
You get a new me every time the sun wakes.
Do I get a new you?

Keep pushing buttons.

What if, one morning, you awaken
to the dull ache of ennui
and my presence bores you?
We'll make up a fight for no apparent reason,
so we can reconcile.

Stir up emotions.

Inquisitiveness is amusing,

over-confidence, endearing.
Insecurity, reassuring.
Get on my nerves and inside my brain.
Slowly crawl into my heart.
Claim it as yours, if it makes you smile.
Claim I'm yours. Perhaps you are right,
or maybe you've just scratched the surface.

Shells

They rushed out of the water and settled in the sand
worn by years, maybe decades of life.
Once sanctuaries, they are now abandoned,
but they don't know the difference.

If you hold them to your ear, you can hear the ocean,
or the cry of emptiness, the dirges of love.
That was not me you met with rough edges.
That was not you I collided with and could not break.

There is sand… on that imaginary beach we didn't visit,
beneath warm waters we never touched.
That was not me swimming against the current.
That was not you causing me hurt.
It was them, now lying in the sand—
dormant and clueless, aging unchanged.

We never got to meet in that blissful silence—
or perhaps we did. It's hard to tell.
You would have liked me…
Those shells, exquisite in their guise,
barely conceal the opulence
of our untouched, uncharted depths.

Essentials

Erase the words, yet spare my pen.
Claim the house, but leave my home.
Spend the passion, but save my love.
Take me in pieces, and leave me whole.

Seize the rocks, but spare the strength.
Indulge beginnings, release the ends.
Unpick the lily, relish its scent.
Take that walk, and let it rain.

Essentials…

Let the world spin.
Let the trees grow.
Let my skin age.

Withhold the happiness, but leave the peace.
Gather the wind, propel the breeze.
Own the change, but leave the moment.
Live the moment, until the end.

The Excuse

I am not your love, the one
who keeps you awake at night,
staring at the ceiling. I am the one
you overlooked when you thought
you could do better. Now you realize
that "better" is about loving, and being loved.

I am the one who speaks up,
unwilling to compromise my worth
for the sake of love. The one
who desired you but left you
free to explore. And explore you did,
alien worlds, shutting me out
at every knock, until you woke up
one morning yearning for more.
The children we never had
stared you in the face, asking why.

So, with your typical confidence,
you knocked on my door
sharing your epiphany, proclaiming
I am your love. I am not your love.
I am the *hiraeth* of a reality you never lived.
I am the one who would not break your heart,
if only you had known.

I am the scalding trickle that burns you
before dissolving into mist.

I am not your love.
I am the excuse not to love.
Please stop using me.
Open your heart and go.

El Maestro

The giant and the sprite hold hands.
As they tread the town streets, dust swirls.
"Is that your daughter? She is growing fast!"

The gentle breeze toys with her golden locks.
Her cosmic forehead glows under the tropical sun.
Her red gingham nylon dress taunts the wind.

I will walk countless miles with you.
I will sweep your church willingly,
if you allow my head to rest on your Santa belly,
if you let me keep the pennies
that escape from your pocket.

I will amble along the seaside boulevard
with you and rediscover your stories.
I will be hushed while you pay homage
to life and beauty, to love and God.

I will match your slower pace,
and treat you to your favorite yogurt.
I will take you to the Yankee game.
I will give you all I possess,
as a token for your love.[9]

---

[9] In Memoriam: B.S.

Symphony of the Goddess

Mother, you channel life.
From a single womb, countless designs.
An empress-priestess, with a power born.
Nature and merit secure your throne.

Mother, through you the source
of love is endless, and pushing forth.
Why through great pain, producing life.
Nurturing goddess, you are divine.

Mother, within your heart
my own heart rests… in peace survives.
For when my days seem bleak and dark,
there you are surely, holding me tight.

If words could tell of such a love;
there'd be one poem retold by all.
That in your arms it is all right.
You are the gift from love, to life.

Dream Garden

When Daisy grows,
our love will stand strong.
When Viola unfolds,
our passion reborn.
When Rubber hardens,
our garden will flourish.

Baby Tears will scamper about,
with silly giggles and crescent eyes.
And your gloves will conquer the yard:
planting, digging, weeding.

I'll gaze through the kitchen window,
teary-eyed, delaying your lunch call
until I revel in a brief respite—

savoring the fruits of my labor,
so precious, so different,
so blessed, so mine.

The Day He Proposed

The immense lake stunned, with eerie blue
waters, where many had met their fate.
Too still to be shallow, too deep for easy escape.

We wore our hopes in white, our fears in red,
and planted them like poppies on the golden hillside.
Air, earth, and water whirled and entwined.

Beneath Dawn Redwood boughs reaching my way,
I sensed the call to climb and embrace serene vistas.
An exultant, dulcet buzz lingered in my ears—

hummingbird feathers tinting each question mark
on the horizon. I almost stumbled as I leaned to grasp
the gem that vied with the adamant sun,

and since I couldn't see, I touched instead:
the elation, the dread, the virtues
and faults of the rugged landscape.

Silence was sweeter than expected,
as we drove home equipped for a journey.

Old Man with the Pipe

I bought an outfit for an event
I will not attend.

I keep waiting for someone,
though "I'll return" was never said.

I keep peeling the orange,
for someone else to enjoy.[10]

I keep sharpening,
yet still not sharp.

I keep desiring,
but lack the wherewithal.

Uncertain about joining you;
how that will go, I simply don't know.

No one who ventured
has returned to give me hope.

Five long years living with your ghost…
you within, you without.

---

[10] In Memoriam: A.S.

Timeless

Time is the shelf life of the irrelevant,
the reckoning of the unimportant,
the marker of the finite.

Sixty counts of self-imposed death sentences,
static as matter, constant as dreams—
blank notebook pages turned by the wind.

For what truly matters is not subject to time,
not a mother's love, nor the sublime;
not gazing into your eyes, not bliss.

Smiles are ageless. Love doesn't seek
permission to exist. What truly is,
requires no reason, measure, or excuse.

Life does not dance to the beat of tick-tock.
To love, time is but a leaf teased by the wind.

Alchemy in Ink

Words spill like pennies from my rucksack,
modest yet priceless, clinking with abundance.
Words are cheap—invaluable.
They architect our existence.

Feelings, bold as *yang*, impregnate the mind,
until thoughts bloom like daffodils
in early Spring. Others wither,
their hues cocooned within.

Yet the mind persists as a perpetual womb:
birthing form, schemes, plots, and plans.
The choice is ours whether to grant them life.

Restless minds, arid minefields,
flirt with emotion to evoke an explosion.
The answer is intrusion, phantoms of illusion
flash-flooding midnight vision.

Words, like infants, start pure and innocent,
maturing within. Infused with our thoughts,
they beget love, home, hate, and war.

But peace does not reside in words.
It dwells in silence. Silence observes
without judgment. It loves without necessity,
converses without speech.

In the beginning, there was "The Word,"
shaping you and me. It lent soul to the formless
and limbs to the unthinkable.
Empires rose, lives crumbled.

My Valentine

I.
My dearest love,

On a whim, the wind delivered you,
to my window, in serenade.
You showed me gardens filled with daisies,
glistening waters, and promenades.
In the distance, hills stole our every breath
with understated grandeur.
We embraced, gazing together,
picturing our own world,
with high peaks, falls,
meadows, and knolls.

My precious one,

Could words convey your goodness
to my soaring heart?
You graze my wings with a soft caress.
Sensing my longing, you left me fly.
My lucid dream, my astral charm;
now that you're here, I need not ask
for love, passion, flowers or songs.
You are my song, my realm of gratitude.
With me at last, my Valentine.

II.
My dear love, as time flows by,
your love augments and multiplies,
with master strokes, you paint as one,
a bit of suede, a bit of shine.

My ardent love, you keep me warm
through icy cold and frigid nights.
Your fire burns with iridescence.
In random places, you light your match.

My lavish love, your gifts I bear
with heavy weight and burden light.
They fill me with anticipation,
plump with hope, teeming with life.

My precious love, my home's your heart,
with ample rooms and lofty heights.
Delicate candles bedeck your halls.
Passion and art enrich your walls.

My lasting love, like fine-aged rum,
you taste fuller every passing month.
Your lips are spirits and sugar cane.
Your fingers pamper my curly mane.

My one true love, give me your hand,
tell me your truths, rest on my lap,
for thrills are exuberant with you by my side.
Oh glory, oh grace, for My Valentine.

Labels

I'm one of those
who folds my socks but don't make my bed,
who wears a cross but chants Om,
who is pro-life but believes in choice.

I'm one of those
who talks a lot but prefers silence,
who cares a lot, and yet not enough,
who has a home but doesn't feel at home,
who feels a void I don't avoid.

Measuring tape won't do you any good.
I will not fit in your cardboard box.
None of your labels spells out my name.

I'm one of those
who wears a gem and hugs a tree,
who flies with birds and bathes with pigs,
who cleans up well but not always cleans up—
who is courageous and cowardly,
self-centered but generous.

I am one who declines to be jailed
by names, ideologies, and "truths."
I refuse to be fooled by the suffering
of this realm, don't care to join
the race to nowhere.

I'm one of those
who has taken life too seriously,
but somehow, not enough.
I'm happiest thinking of existence
as an illusion, a fleeting dream.

Save your judgement for tactile things.
Use your breath for a deep inhale;
or to cool a cup of tea.

Wear your own cross; or share my Om.
As you come in, leave your shoes
and labels at the door.

Unconditional

Love me when there is nothing to love.
When my hair has thinned,
when I'm no longer thin.
Love me when it's inconvenient.
When you can't see me or count on me.
Love me beyond reciprocity.
When you get neither the comfort
of my company nor the passion of intimacy.

Love me when there is nothing left to say,
when all has been spoken and words are useless.
Love me when I least expect it,
when the story has been told,
when the bridges have been burnt.

Love me like air is present, with certainty,
without noise. Love me in quietude,
in the things that need no words.
Love me in action, through time and space.
Love me when you can no longer count,
when your eyes cease to see.

Love me with the silence of a thousand spaces,
with the patience of a dwindling creek.
Love me if our paths reach the same mountain,
and if there is no mountain, please love me, still.
Love me the only way love loves:
today, tomorrow, unconditionally.

Of Bliss Untold

Stroll in quiet contentment,
cascading from the unknown—

a smile born of letting go
of unnecessary objects.

The once solid barrier of emptiness
now turns porous at the mere glimpse of you.

Bliss, on a crisp evening,
flooding your eyes with joy…

Nirvana, in the face of loss.

Crying Shoulder

When I cry, you speak
of faith, hope, and surrender.
You talk about the good to come,
in divine timing, of resting
in the arms of Source:
content, anticipating, present.

When you speak, I cry.
You know of all I desired and never received.
You understand being denied,
things small and large.
Rejection is protection, and all that.

You yearn to bring me joy,
buying the music I like,
making my favorite dish:
braised eggplant with black-bean rice.
Does God get tired of your constant nagging,
that I get what I want?

One day I will learn.
I'll be more like you.
Can you ship me a year's worth of wisdom,
and a comforting hug,
a jar of ground annatto seeds,
and coconut fudge?

You claim I'm delicate,

and you would know.
How I wish I could fall apart
in your arms—the arms that swaddle me
with endless tenderness.

Taste of Salt

Melodic

I rock my baby to Iron & Wine,
thinking of times lying supine
on the floor of Madera's warmth,
a laptop snoozing to mellow vibes.

Now I see love, lost in my head,
reliving those days.
Freedom, golden roads,
coming home with a bag of Sol Food,
moments of silence,
with boredom lightly strewn.
It was more than okay.
Carefree and riant, you'd sing, sing, sing.

Now I see love, watching you sing
as you played guitar.
Best of friends, oh love.
Gone from my life like broken crystal.
Now I keep you, love,
locked with my valuables,
my diamond ring.
In my heart, oh love,
safe to remember any time of need.

There I keep you, love.
It brings me smiles and sets me free
from the confines, oh love,
filled with duties, and musts, and ifs.

My mind flies away to simpler times,
a stretch, a kiss. Don't forget me, love.
Iron & Wine, music, bliss, bliss, bliss…

Therapeutic

Like a brush of new pigment on an aging canvas,
your love rejuvenates.

Like a sip of freshly brewed tea on a busy morning,
your love revitalizes.

Like a cluster of blooms in an empty room,
your love beautifies.

Like stones in a stream, filtering flowing water,
your love cleanses.

Like glimpsing candy through a child's eyes,
your love excites.

Like a tender embrace from the most caring arms,
your love comforts.

Like a dash of salt on pristine white rice,
your love enhances.

Like a vacant gaze at a breathtaking sight,
your love soothes.

Like a subtle eye-roll,
your love says volumes without uttering a word.

Like a sincere, warm smile,

your love is uplifting.

Like knowing there is no tomorrow,
your love is pure presence.

Like my grandmother's hands,
your love heals.

Prayer for an Angel

Now you glance from afar
at the ones you once held near,
tears in your eyes, consumed by regret.

The gifts you squandered,
your untapped intellect…

You look on silently, feeling unworthy
of all you once had—
at those you mistreated, fooled,
thinking you didn't really need them.

You had it all, and you pissed it away.
You had them all, and you pushed them away.
You wanted it all, now you're wasting away.

I pray for you, Angel, and I cry
knowing you've cried,
for your hurt is my hurt,
for my wish is your redemption.

Can you reclaim what you once had?

Grateful, this time. Careful, this time.
Life believes in second chances,
but it takes courage to ask.

Losing You

Missing you
is hearing your drums
when I play my guitar.
It's picturing curls
as I drive in my car.
It's gasping for air;
it's battling the wind.

Having you
is sweetly fictitious
for truth is a bummer;
as actual as Olaf
in the dead of summer.
It is fleeting; it's deceiving.

Loving you
is fantastic and simple,
excruciating and sore.
It's wishing all remained
as it had been before.
It's knowing. It's going.

Losing you
is being a river reluctant to flow;
getting uninvited and still wanting to go.
It is unfitting and yet somehow fair.
Like being hung… by a nun.

Safe

In your arms, I find breath.
On your chest, I can rest.

Your words dissolve my discomfort.
Within your borders, I tread.

To your rhythm, I dance freely.
With your tunes, I sing boldly.

Looking in your direction,
I stare vacant at the sea.

You're immense!

In your vast waters, I swim,
and your roar is solely mine.

In your depths, I expand.
Worries dissipate, sorrow fades away.

In your cosmos, I find time.
In your shadowlands, I test my boundaries,

and in your haven, I feel…
safe.

Amber Mantra

I kept your letter, all four pages of stringing beads,
because "anything worth saying is worth repeating,"
you said.

A mantra, recited over and over
until it wills you into a trance…
"I love you. I love you? I love you!"

A fragile note turned sepia from golden ink.
Your parting gift of thanks: undying fondness,
and a breath that is always deep.

For one who is truly loved is always loved.
I will not ask the present to affirm the past.

I'll reread your letter, instead,
and wear this feeling preserved in amber.
Your words, dry resin and hardened seconds,
a pendant warming my heaving chest.

"I love you. I love you? I love you!"
Like a mantra, soothing, if seldom read.

Romance is a Garment

Romance is a garment in a washing machine,
It needs the right setting and temperature
to be cleaned. With frequent washes,
colors will fade. The fabric might shrink;
or it could even fray.

But if it proves hardy, withstands the test
of time, it becomes a second skin,
a glove that fits just right. Years pass,
fibers unravel, bringing about holes.
Rips reveal that usage has taken its toll.

Eventually, the old garment
must be thrown away. Not a problem!
You can find it at the store or eBay.
But it's been discontinued,
no use hitting the road.
So you wish you'd been more careful
with the settings and the mode.

Out you go, out of habit,
to find a new one to mold.
Not as pretty, not as comfortable,
but give it time, and it might work.

Hindsight 20/20

Had I known it would sting so much,
I wouldn't have torn you from my heart.
You are the sore that never heals,
that burns anew with every scratch.

I would have carried you everywhere I went,
had I known you would follow anyway.
You've journeyed continents with me,
sampled every taste, seen all the sights,
witnessed every breath, enjoyed every night.

You are the first to know when things go
right, the ever-ready shoulder when I need
to cry. And though you're not here,
you never left my side.

A futile battle against love...
You're ever present, in hindsight.

Damaged Goods

Where are you, damaged goods?
Is it nice out there?
Life support cut you short.
You weren't that rare.

Torment has ceased. Now deceased…
Do you get to watch?
Was heaven worth the arduous life?
Have you become a star?

> *Suffering is a magnet*
> *for those who ache*
> *but arid is the land of pain.*
> *Clarity is freedom;*
> *compassion, a choice.*
> *Self-destruction is vain.*

I'll always wonder what you were like
behind the veil of anguish.
I'll always know that you were mine
until the day you languished[11].

Send me a smile. I passed you along,
but you held no resentment.
Ship me a blessing from the eternal seas.
Sail in the joy that mends me.

---

[11] In Memoriam: M.R.G.

Positive

You ask if I love you. Let me count the ways:

I love you like I cherish a deep breath—
always available, but oh,
it feels exquisite when taken.

I love you like I appreciate clean air,
sometimes needing distance to truly find it.
I love you akin to morning coffee:
consumed daily, yet never taken for granted.

I love you in the manner I enjoy roses:
with their enchantment and thorns;
the way I embrace yoga—
growing stronger, more serene.

I love you like tea, smooth and sultry;
like the four seasons: ever-changing,
yet unwavering.

I love you akin to Stinson Beach,
Crater Lake, Lucas Valley,
when you sleep, when you laugh,
your nature laid bare.

I love you as I did yesterday—
assuredly more, and only increasing.

Exposé

If you truly knew me, you would know
I speak my mind and scribe my heart.
I seldom wear my favorite color,
and don a smile when I'd rather cry.

That the water runs deeper, its clarity
deceiving, and while I relish simple joys,
simplicity does not define me.

You would know I favor people over dogma,
and silence over people.
That I'd love to have five lives
and live them all—simultaneously.

That I misplaced my soul atop a mountain,
seeking every crevice ever since.
I left my joy in a bus by *Hato Viejo*
watching cows graze a rolling hill.

That I left my heart at *Playa Rincón*,
captured in a bikini's frame.
When I close my eyes, I envision Eagle's Bay,
and from China Camp, the Richmond Bridge.

You would note I prize friendships
above possessions, and nothing above tranquility.
That I strive for balance on a yoga mat
and find solace in a cup of tea.

That my cross is so nimble,
it's sometimes a burden.
That I left my love bathing by the sea,
close my eyes and see it every morning.

Clearing

I see you,
>meandering
>>like a river through rocks—
>like baking soda
through the muck,
cleansing.

I feel you,
>the familiar sting
>>of a heart scrape,
>a pull to relapse
into a drunken phase—
unchecked.

I sit with you,
>unquestioning motives.
>>Invitations are realized,
>dates with destiny
are needed to provide…
clarity.

I release you.
>I can't build
>>on a foundation that never was.
>It's pointless to rehash
a broken past;

absurd to indulge what won't satisfy—anymore.

Becoming

I cradle poetry in my arms—
unblemished innocence born
from the lives I have lived,
from the loves I have loved.

Rushing waves of wonder
cascade from my pen,
with streaks of yesterday's sepia,
and tomorrow's vivid red.

I am the restless sea,
blue's incessant cadence:
depths, waves, shores,
rocks and endless skies.

Poetry flows within me
in moments of stillness
from visions that delight,
and stunning, moving sights.

Marvel pools in my bones
from the goodness I have known,
and in blissful existence—
I am, I become.

Taste of Salt

Between the Ears

The silence is deafening; the pause, enduring.
Thoughts starve in a fruitless brain, abject.
They inch toward each other,
only to wither before coherence dawns.

There's nothing to say, no tears to shed;
nothing to regret, no one to blame.
Owning and knowing in dreadful reticence...
Exactly where you are supposed to be,
with whom you're supposed to be,
doing what you should be.

A life made by design: your own...
No reason to weep, no fingers to point.
Crickets run the night. For company,
nothing but a keyboard.

Little Victories

With you, my love, it's in the subtle moments:

a toothless smile, a hushed yawn,
a heart-warming gaze, a home tour,
a stroller glide on a balmy afternoon,

midnight conversations, eyes that stray,
slumber through the night, a contented face,
a soothing bath, fingers through your hair.

With you, my love, it's an array of smiles;
big milestones fade away,
as the small triumphs stretch for miles.

Rojita

I left you by the sea-side boulevard
after a night of embraces.
Ended our fling with a phone call,
refused to follow your traces.

Thailand was too distant, as was Knoxville.
Your hair club seemed out of place,
and my patience ran out quickly
when you found it hard to touch base.

Your angelic portrait faded fast
as your attitude gained a few pounds.
Spoonfuls of intimacy left me hungry
when passion craved encore rounds.

For a marriage is no open house
and from bliss, you needed a break,
you may call me *Rojita*, heartbreaker—
the sweet, feisty one who got away.

What I Prefer Over You

A tranquil evening, a sunset's glow
How sunlight ponders on the water's flow

A sublime melody sung by a bird
An old, tired thought, scarcely heard

A serene, sandy beach, untouched by thunder
Turquoise waters, deep in slumber

Hearing bold words in nature's quiet hum
Inhaling deeply, letting moments come

A satisfying stretch, extending my stay
Hiking uphill in a rugged landscape

Snowy days, a world clad in white
A hot cup of tea, warming me inside

Watching free-range cows graze in the field
California's happy cows, their smile revealed

Sleeping the day, a peaceful reprieve
Staying home with nothing to achieve

Reading under my throw, sans expectations
Witnessing the freedom of a bird migration

A delectable meal to nourish my bones

An afternoon bike ride in the warm sun

Seeing an old friend who makes me laugh
Lavender and ylang-ylang in my bubble bath

Escaping the world for a secluded getaway
Showering in the rain on a Caribbean day

What We Know

Who are you? I hesitate to guess.
Conjectures won't bring us any closer.
Where my path leads, you can't foresee.
No "X" marks the spot on my blurred,
scratched-up map.

You are the still, obscure lake,
where I once feared swift, silent drowning.
I, the risky ocean, warm yet untamed.
You dreaded the wrath
of my brisk tidal waves.

Meanwhile, the tail-wagging Earth
pants and smirks—alive and aware,
mocking our claim to ownership
while we ride her fur.
We, conceited fleas, observers and observed—
playing dual roles in aimless soliloquies.

What are we, then? Could it be we are just
life-size bobbleheads adorned with question
marks? Where are you? Who am I?
What good are questions? We only know
the bounds of our comprehension.

Taste of Salt

Serendipity's Tango

Walking these streets, it's déjà vu.
I've wandered here before, *si señor*.
Sipped this fine wine once, oh yes!
Intoxicating… never more than now.

Change is here: yesterday, today, tomorrow.
I strive to keep pace as it strides briskly ahead.
I may rest on this bench, while it plots its course—
but then it goes rogue, it whirls
in a tango entwining its legs around mine.

And you… who are you?
Your name eludes me, yet I know you.
Seemingly fun; are you?
Kinda skinny, kinda handsome…
May I kiss you? Why doesn't everyone?

And here we stand.
I must drag you and your rightful choices.
Why the defiance?
Or is it help you offer?

Let's go for a hike—
twirl around the grass like in the movies.
You appear sane; has your mind drifted?
What mind? You question.

Eternally Young

You rest on your head,
flawless and delicate,
with an innocent face
and that blank, harmless gaze.
You lay on your head
and your firm legs bounce
up and over...
Your gray hair defies logic—
for you are beautifully strong;
you are eternally young.

Rest Stop

I've sealed myself in this furnished cavern,
where familiar objects offer solace.
With a flickering candle as the only witness,
it's time to review my deeds.

I turn the page, exhaling, resetting my chi.
Recalling my truth, I learn from silence,
having uttered so much.
From this mighty throne, I ponder
what gifts to give, which ones to withhold.

This agile current carries me
from end to end of the river beyond,
zigzagging and back again.
Stop! Let me catch my breath.

Yoga my body from the bottom up.
Hose off my gown, scrub away the dirt,
massage these muscles and get them ready
to lift the weight of another day.

Spring

I tread these hilly streets, my will a testament.
Manicured azaleas mumble, "Let me be."

Yes, the warmth is inviting,
but Caribbean souls won't get reparations

in the form of blossoming trees
for enduring winter.

In moments of pondering life's unfairness,
the crisp air grants me a glimpse.

Spring paints itself on windy slopes,
where a magnolia opens to the sun.

For Practical Reasons

My breath turns to sighs when I see your face,
yet practical reasons convince me to stay:

You grip the wheel through the neon-lit town,
your clear eyesight guides us once the sun goes down.

Savoring flavors, from Caribbean to Thai,
we sway to ethnic rhythms when spirits are high.

Differences draw us with magnetic force.
Your thoughts, deep and measured, a logical source.

Your purposeful silence isn't born of shyness.
Your fireworks mind, a realm of pure brightness.

You are not a mirror reflecting my stance
but a kindred soul, a fateful dance.

Shuffling the deck on our fool's journey,
resilient and brave, even when it's stormy.

You shield my legs when wind chills bite,
checking on me when we're out of sight.

You feed me, you jest, get me pleasantly drunk,
and don't take it personally when I'm in a funk.

You cherish my cooking, finding no wrongs.

You take life in stride, and write me love songs.

I like your sharp wit, and fair credit score,
your plush, queen-sized bed, and boho decor.

Conscientious spenders, rejecting the trends,
we choose simple pleasures, adventures that transcend.

You seek to change the world, passion in your drive.
Though in different ways, we chase the same light.

Excuses

Your letters seep through the hollowed-out Sequoia,
decaying rapidly in our carefree past.
I smirk at your grandiose, rehearsed stories
that exude an air of nonchalance.

I tuck your speech about enlightenment
under a rock I noticed as I lit my path.
It wasn't happiness I sought within you.
There is nothing I gave you I desire back.

Thank you for that…

Don't give me any excuses.
They weren't needed then;
I don't want them now.

Don't point the way.
When you were going,
I was coming back.

Uncomplicated

Softer, your hands, tender upon me,
kneading our smooth romance like dough.
Bliss spills and runs across the floor—
a peaceful sway, a gentle wring,
a hint of friction.

Let's not diminish this peace,
the nonexistent drama of the uncomplicated.
Shall I find amusement
at the cost of your smile?
Should I engage in mind games
as winter draws near?

Not with you, not today.
Egos may throw tantrums when we decline
to ride their roller coaster of chaos;
but I've matured and prefer simplicity.

What a draw, this quiet evening,
a hug without sparks.
It's Friday night. Let's stay home
and enjoy this lukewarm fire,
a cup of tea— a fiction book
under the blanket, just you and me.

Yoga Therapy

Your body speaks,
and as you listen,
body parts articulate.

Aching shoulder? Overburdened.
Tense thighs? Emotional heist.
Dry calves yearn for lotion.

For the remedies: Butterfly,
Thread the Needle,
let things slide.

For a sore chest?
Compassion… and flower tea
in generous rations.

Disclaimer:
No medical advice intended.
Hope no doctors were offended.

Nursing New Beginnings

Such is life with its twists and turns,
if you're flexible, it will have you bend.
If you're rigid, it will see you break.

Such is change with its taste for loss,
for leaving behind habits and friends,
and learning uncertainty where sureness has been.

And the dense clouds parked in my brain
shall lift with winter and dissolve in rain.
Spring will dawn a clear horizon and grow:

new roots, new friends, new trails to walk,
new flowers to plant, new love to gain,
and a new life to raise, in the nursery

that is my heart, our garden, and her room,
just the same. Each day, a new bloom—
every wish, a new realm.

The Things We Carry

A chandelier,
a wine rack,
a Buddha statue;

a second thought,
a bulky table,
an old book,
a useless feeling,
a piggy bank,

and the hope that one day
we'll unload it all
and have free hands—

to collect more
to leave behind…

The Calling

What do you seek from me?
The clamor has faded.
Now, only a dazed, honeycomb cloud
wanders through the vastness.
At times, it lets light shine through;
at others, it obscures the firmament.

What is my purpose?
I am ripe and ready. I'm all dressed up,
my hair styled, and we have a rendezvous.
Where are you leading me?
What will be served? How can I help?
Is anyone listening?

My ears are attentive, my eyes keen,
my heart's an open valve. My arms stretch
to the ether, embracing the wind.
I am that leaf twirling with the breeze.
Where do we go from here?
Where do I alight when the gusts subside?

With eyes sealed, clouds dispersed,
and breath drawn in, I ask:
What is my calling?

Taste of Salt

Addicted to the Chase

You snore loudly, draped in jadedness,
in a dream where my presence slowly fades.
Once the chase concludes,
indifference takes root.

You smile as you sip your own sweat,
jogging on the bachelor hamster wheel.
But soon, even that circular track will close.

It's Tuesday night, and the un-intoxicating wine,
mixed with my bitterness, begets weariness.
We've walked this path before.
What's left for me to prove?

Apathy ensnares us both with sticky claws.
If my harmonies don't resonate,
seek your echoes beyond my door.

Indifference, the telltale sign
that illusion is gone.

Scratches

I shed the tough veneer on the way in.
Scars protrude my body like phantom limbs.
With every rebirth, a new fragility—
each dermal layer is just as thin.

When will clarity dawn?

Endurance eludes the weary, old skin,
persistently enduring a cycle within.
In vain, it sheds and glazes its outer layer,
forever growing frail, slight, and prim.

When will it learn?
When will I learn?

Blazing Hums

I rest at the crest of your peak, opening
my home, so you may enter, dream,
and awaken. Instinct soaring inside my veins,
lips part, pleasure echoes. I sip the full cup
of your mouth; a crescendo. I long to close
my eyes but keep them open—
a blatant overload of you, my sole focus.

You drink from my mouth, the tempo rises.
I serve myself not merely to give,
but to receive. A surround sound melody
wisps from the ground, engulfing us,
a blazing rainbow. Hummingbirds buzz,
cardinals chirp their most vibrant hue
over the flames. I sit in the fire of your feast,
surrendering in the highest of grounds.

Unforeseen

In a quest for scissors,
the missing pendant appeared.
You served me a bright smile
when all I ordered was beer.

I was browsing for Pantene
when Matrix crossed my aisle;
gazing at softboy mannequins
when I noticed your rugged style.

Random seed, love,
sprouting in unexpected spaces.
Once you find it, it stays.
Pick your subject, it won't fade.

Oblivious, it doesn't seek,
yet in its silence, emotions peak.
Curious seed, love,
growing orchids over dead wood.

How Soon They Forget

Words once spoken, promises made
Shared journeys, laughing unrestrained
Bonfires danced, takeout on Tuesday night
Exotic trips under the moonlight

Good intentions, being "there"
Calling to tell me you still care
Movies, songs, a turbulent plane ride
Unplanned adventures, an off-country drive

Hair, legs, lips entwined
Knowing that you were only mine
A phantom, a silhouette, a ghost
Amazing how soon they forget.

Green

Green, the hue of peace and tranquility,
inhaling deeply, marveling on a prairie's vast expanse,
gazing at mountains and the distant horizon.

A harbinger of hope, the assurance that life
follows its course, endures, and multiplies.
It is sustenance, and crops, anticipating
imminent blooms.

It is the shade of beginnings, not fully knowing,
yet persisting… of smiles free from cynicism—
of war and camouflage, land, and deception.

Green, the reflection in your staring eyes,
contemplating the unthinkable, toppling
others in its wake. Don't shut them.

Green, the emblem of growth, the hue
of an expectant earth, innocence, deceit, power,
promise, tickers, danger… and you.

Purpose

Show me destination,
for long is the journey
of those who ignore it.

Show me venues,
for fruitful are talents
only when used.

Show me path,
for myriad are the ways,
countless the possibilities.

Show me partners,
for wealth or poverty
are best shared.

Show me timing,
for life is both too long
and not long enough.

Show me Purpose.

If Only...

If I knew you missed me,
I would wonder why you don't tell me.
If you were to tell me,
I would say, "Do something about it."
If you did something about it,
we would have to start over.
If we did started over, we might hurt each other.
If I hurt again, I might forget you missed me.

If love were enough, we'd be together.
If love were enough, there would be no wonder.
What if you sang me unheard-of songs?
What if you wrote me untold letters?
What if our best was saved for last?
I wish you would surprise me and prove me wrong.

If only feelings ran like rivers.
If only we had no feelings.
If onlys are many,
If onlys are all we have left.

Dead Weight

Amor, I've carried you with me
too far, for too long.
You won't walk beside me,
and my arms are sore.
I'm putting you down,
and letting you be.
One moves faster
unburdened, free.

Alignment

Two slender bodies, bare,
lie in repose, spent after.
Familiar echoes, now enhanced.
Carefree giving, a mellow flow,
untroubled breath.

In your hands, in your arms,
tame waters, fire and earth.
Pure sensations, an erotic mire—
swamp life and pristine lakes.

Peace in the passion,
a hushed, humble bliss.
Let's refrain from labeling,
and repeat.

You Never Call Me by my Name

"You never cloak yourself around me.
Your voice sounds strange.
Something changed. What's wrong?"

This growing distance stretches
like a sleepy jaguar between us.
Nostalgia may blindfold us
yet our hearts can't deceive us.

You detect a tinge less tenderness
with each uttered word.
Even when it's over, you know me.
Even when it's over… baby.

Alphabet

Absent love
Baffling love
Cold love
Detached love
Empty love
Fruitless love
Gone love
Heartless love
Indifferent love
Joyless love
Kept love
Lost love
Missing love
Neglected love
Oblivious love
Proud love
Questioned love
Rebound love
Silent love
Torn love
Unyielding love
Vanished love
Withheld love
eXtinguished love
Yearning love
Zealous love

Your love is not love.

Talk to You

Fogged windows speak to you,
muted sorrows echo of you.
Paralyzed beings ache for your touch,
Heart and soul call for you.
Come to me, unlike the first time:
a timid feline, scarred, rebounding.
Come to me, aware, open, wise.

Come to me, love that's ever-fresh,
potent, tender.
Come to me and say nothing,
or pour your heart,
for I'll embrace every word,
as long as it is from you.
Take everything, as long as it arrives.

Come to me. Stay.

You, He

His eyes are blue, yours hazel.
He is breath; you, butterflies.
His hair is curly, yours straight.
He's young; you, younger.
He's stable; you're scattered.
He's committed; you, flaky.
He's free; you're a prisoner.
He embraces; you dodge.
He is muscles; you, fun.
He gives; you withhold.
He's tall; you, short.
He's big; you, small.
He's subtle; you, overpowering.
He's intuitive; you, logical.
He is tactile; you, too.
He allows; you control.
He's quiet; you, loud.
He's amused; you, scared.
He is home; you, street.
He's naive; you, cunning.
He's tender; you, cute.
He's oral; you, too.
He's confident; you, hesitant.
He's out; you're in.
He's out; you're out.

Taste of Salt

Open

Open
Door, heart, legs
Lips, arms, life

Come
Now, later, tomorrow
Someday, never

Leave
Now, later, tomorrow
Someday, never

Embraced by Flowers

Days ascend, and twilight dawns
on a proud sunflower in my vase,
seeking the sun's guiding light.
Spotting him at last, she flirts,
brimming with crimson smiles.
She's a mother, life teeming in her seed head.

A most desired gardenia, demure yet bold,
discreet in color, bold in aroma.
Her message loud as you approach my door:
she's a girl, here to have fun.
The audience claps as she reveals her scent,
capturing it in their hands, a natural perfume.

Dreamy daisy, aglow in my moon garden.
Glistening petals weave a lush, pure melody.
I hear their murmur outside my window,
waving until one notices me.
I ask them to reserve a spot in their choir.

Wind-kissed and proud, Camellia's resilient
blooms jewel my winter garden. Arriving
when others retreat, adversity fuels her roots.
Glossy foliage, a green delight,
even in the dead of summer.

My life, cocooned in daily petals,
and seasonal scents— an aromatic symphony.

More Poetry by Antonia:

Love Bites: Poetry & Prose

In her debut collection, Antonia serves enticing bites that whip the day into a sweet confection. Every carefully crafted poem samples the intricate flavors of the heart, ruminated by the mind on its quest for home.

Hindsight 2020: Brief Reflections on a Long Year

Hindsight 2020 takes you by the hand into a reflective and hopeful space, after years of unprecedented change. Delve into love and loss, change and reinvention with grace and insight.

Palette: Love Poems and Painted Words

Experience evocative portraits, moving landscapes, and intimate still lifes of the inner world. Palette layers and blends love poems and nature odes with vibrant colors and a variety of poetic elements, including rhythm and subtle rhyme, exquisite imagery, and inventive wordplay. Black and white illustrations pepper this unforgettable poetry collection.

Things I Could Have Said in One Line But Didn't

An emotional journey of reflection, introspection, and wonder at the complexities of life and love. This moving poetry collection delves into longing, relationships, and the human condition. A sense of intimacy and contemplation weaves nature, experience, and the inner world into carefully crafted poems that reveal how self-inquiry can help you grow, heal, and live more authentically.

Antonia's books are available on Amazon, Apple Books, Barnes & Noble, Kobo, other book sellers, and library apps.

About the Author

Antonia Wang has written several poetry collections in English and Spanish, including Love Bites, In the Posh Cocoon, *Matices*, Palette, and Things I Could Have Said in One Line But Didn't. She is an international CASS scholar originally from the Dominican Republic.

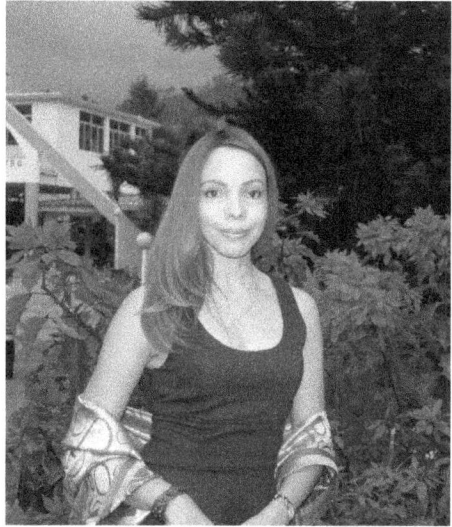

Her poetry is known for its vibrant imagery and thoughtful exploration of love, loss, personal transformation, and identity. Her distinctive poetic voice appears in various journals and anthologies.

Antonia draws inspiration from her world travels, Caribbean heritage, and 20-year yoga practice. She lives with her family in the United States.

Website: biteslove.com

Acknowledgments

The original versions of some of these poems were first published on my old poetry blog "For What It's Worth" and on my website "biteslove.com." They have since been removed.

Thank you to Vanessa Anderson of Night Owl Freelance for thoughtfully editing this poetry collection.

I am deeply grateful to my family for supporting me on my writing journey and providing a wonderful place for reflection and mindfulness.

Thank you to all my readers, new and old! Your feedback and encouragement inspire my writing. I hope that my poetry can evoke emotions, spark reflection, and accompany you on your journey of self-discovery.

www.ingramcontent.com/pod-product-compliance
Lightning Source LLC
Chambersburg PA
CBHW051732040426
42447CB00008B/1087